CADZOW-HACZOW BOOKS

A POCKET GUIDE TO A MINDFUL LIFE

Martin Stepek was born in Scotland, at Cambuslang near Glasgow on 19 February 1959. He started writing while at school but never sought to publish. Instead he began his career as a company director in his father's family business. It was not until 2012 at the age of 53 that he published his first book, the epic poem *For There is Hope*, followed by *Mindful Living* (2014), *Mindful Poems* (2015) and *Mindful Living 2* (2015). He collaborated online with the Polish-American poet John Guzlowski, resulting in their joint volume of micro poems *Waiting for Guzlowski* (2017). His latest works are *A Pocket Guide to a Mindful Life* (2018) and *Steps to a Mindful Life* (2018).

By the same author

For There is Hope
Mindful Living
Mindful Poems
Mindful Living 2
Waiting for Guzlowski
A Pocket Guide to a Mindful Life
Steps to a Mindful Life

MARTIN STEPEK

A Pocket Guide to a Mindful Life

CADZOW-HACZOW BOOKS

CADZOW-HACZOW BOOKS

Published in Cadzow-Haczow Books 2018

Printed in Great Britain
Copyright © Martin Stepek 2018

Contents

How to use this book....8

What matters? 9

Understand this deeply - your mind automatically develops destructive traits....10

Understand this deeply - your mind is poor at paying attention and wanders constantly....13

What is Mindfulness?....15

Mindfulness helps us see our unreliable mind in real time....17

Mindfulness helps us defuse or neutralise our destructive mental traits....19

Mindfulness develops our strength of focus and attention on the moment....21

Mindfulness helps us develop great mental qualities in the long term....22

How to do Mindfulness and become more mindful....23

Three methods of developing your mind....26

A summary....28

How to use this Book

I have written and designed this book to be the closest thing to a guide for living your life as I can manage to create.

The idea is for you to read and re-read it regularly, so that the fundamental insights about yourself, your mind, and how to master it, are within easy reach wherever you are, and whatever is going on at any time in your life.

It's the kind of helpful tool or guide that I truly wish I had had when I was a young adult, and especially in the early years of my mindfulness practice.

I hope you find this book a powerful reminder of what really matters in your life, and a reminder to keep on top of living mindfully. The more you do so the happier you will be, and the more fulfilled will be your precious life.

What Matters?

The purpose of this booklet is to help you live each moment as fully, enjoyably, and kindly as possible.

We have only one life. It is a precious opportunity to experience being alive. We have many senses and we have remarkable intelligence and imagination. With practice and development we can combine these gifts with the skills of mindfulness and wisdom to enjoy a wonderful life, moment by moment. And we can learn not to harm ourselves or others as we do so.

All we have is one precious moment at a time. Regardless of the circumstances, good, bad or indifferent, our task must surely be to make the most of it.

Understand this Deeply – Your Mind Automatically Develops Destructive Traits

Our minds have evolved over eons, and by the remarkable process of chance genetic mutations and fortuitous circumstances through those many millennia, we have developed certain very powerful traits that for long periods helped protect and save us from the myriad of nature's potential dangers. Thus caution, concern, anxiety and other traits surely helped us stay alive as a species, as did aggressive or violent reactions to perceived threats. Even cowering in fear and uncertainty, or laying low after a traumatic experience will have helped us recover in due course.

However many of these traits, such as anger, resentment, hatred, depression, anxiety, stress, poor self-image and other negative habits of mind, now seem to simply get in the way of us enjoying our everyday life. Because these types of emotions and moods grew in strength and frequency as a result of their power to keep us alive in times of danger, they are now far more powerful and dominant than our positive traits. Think about this for a moment. An enjoyable day is great at the time, but mostly forgotten about within a day or so. A bad day however is an experience that we often remember and bring up in conversation sometimes years, even decades later. And this is especially so for terrible life experiences, whereas wonderful life experiences seem much weaker in comparison. This is called negativity bias in psychology.

So our minds, while astonishingly versatile and helpful, are also very unreliable. We often simply don't know when the next negative reaction is going to appear in it. Moreover, we seem to have little control over destructive emotions when they do arise. Lifelong grudges, suicidal thoughts, deep rooted prejudices can bed down in our minds and arise seemingly at random. These often harm our relationships with others but we know through a series of studies that negative emotions also trigger hormonal reactions which in the long term wear out our bodies, causing us to age faster, and die younger.

We should therefore focus hard on embedding the understanding that our minds are not to be trusted, and need mastered, as best we can do this.

Even more importantly, when your mind is disturbed, is feeling low, desolate, that life is pointless, try to remember the major truth that the products of the mind are simply that, products of the mind. They do not reflect your reality; they just seem to. They are like a psychedelic drug making you feel life is a certain way, when in fact life just is. It is up to us to determine how to feel about life, and it is always wisest to try to develop in our minds moods or feelings that we know create good mental and physical health.

So do not believe your mind when it paints the world and your life as negative or pointless.

Understand this Deeply – Your Mind is Poor at Paying Attention, and Wanders Constantly

In order to achieve what we want with our lives, whether that's just enjoying the sunshine on a warm day, or seeking to make a great breakthrough in some field of endeavour, we need to be focussed. Unfortunately the human mind has evolved to be easily distracted. A study by Harvard University in 2012 showed that on average a person's mind wanders from where the person wanted it to be a huge 47% of the time.

Thus almost half of our waking life is spent with our minds having gone off on some mental excursion not of our choosing. Now some of these may be enjoyable – a pleasant daydream – or even beneficial – a new idea for an invention, a business venture, or a work of art. But most are sadly not of much use according to the research. Our distractions tend to be focussed on negative things like past mishaps or errors of judgement, or worries about the future.

This means that the time we could have spent doing what we actually want to do gets lost, a whopping amount every day. Moreover much of what is lost can be the little joys of life that we have noticed so often we forget how pleasant they are. The joy of drinking cold water to quench our thirst. The pleasure of just walking from one place to another. The sight of nature all around us and above us in the sky.

So we need to remember this too; that our minds wander constantly, wasting our precious life and time that could have brought us so much more joy and pleasure, or brought us closer to our life dreams. Again, let this insight deepen inside you so we have the motivation to try to master our minds with mindfulness.

What is Mindfulness?

There are two answers to the question, What is Mindfulness? One describes the process we do which is called mindfulness. That's very simple. Mindfulness is the skill of deliberately noticing what's going on moment by moment. We have this skill in our mind but it's usually not very well developed. Some people, notably artists and poets, have a naturally high level of mindfulness, often called heightened awareness. We can all develop it to a high level.

The second, more important answer to the question, What is Mindfulness?, is this. Mindfulness is a specific skill through which we can cope with our most harmful or painful states of mind, and make the most of the pleasant and positive states of mind as they arise.

As we have noted above we are not good at paying attention so we miss much that is pleasing to our mind, and we lose precious time during which we could be more effectively doing what we actually want to do with our lives. Moreover we have many emotions and moods which cause hurt and anguish, which poisons our moments and in the long run wear us out physically while becoming ingrained habits mentally.
So we can think of the skill of mindfulness as potential antidotes to these poor traits of the mind.

Mindfulness Helps us see our Unreliable Mind in Real Time

As we develop our own mindfulness through practicing it as much as we can in everyday life, we get better at noticing what's actually going on in each moment. Mostly that is about seeing what we see more clearly through our eyes, or hearing sounds more distinctively. This is because our eyes and ears are the most powerful of our senses.

However one of the most important areas where our developing mindfulness helps us most is in noticing much more clearly and frequently what is being created by our mind. Our mind has developed over millions of years to become a constant thinking and reacting machine. It hardly ever stops producing thoughts, responses, ideas, likes, dislikes, daydreams, memories, thoughts of the future.

Some of these automatically created thoughts and reactions are not in our own interest, or not in the interests of the people around us. We've all experienced overreacting to an event. We've all experienced boredom, sadness, unhappiness, loneliness, anger, frustration, or irritation.

These are just some of the unhelpful things that the mind produces without our consent.

The more we practice mindfulness the more we are able to notice what the mind produces, and if it is unhealthy, unhelpful, likely to produce a negative outcome, we are now at least in a position to consider what we can do about the reaction in our mind before it makes us do something destructive.

So mindfulness helps us become very aware of the activities of our mind.

Mindfulness Helps us Defuse or Neutralise our Destructive Mental Traits

There is an old piece of advice uttered to people when someone gets angry. "Just take a deep breath". And when the angry person is very perturbed the phrase is extended to "Just take a deep breath and count to ten". This is perfect mindfulness.

Firstly become aware of your mood. Developing the skill of mindfulness helps us do this.

Then, on noticing that our mind has created a destructive or toxic feeling or thought we decide not to indulge such creations of the mind. To get rid of them we need some time so that they may diminish and fade away naturally, rather than be suppressed.

Focussing on our breath – or some other pleasant and simple subject – takes our attention subtly away from our negative mindset, and in following the breath allows sufficient time to pass so that the mood inside our mind passes and dissipates.

The more frequently we recognise these moods and emotions as they arise, the better we get at knowing how to disarm them through this and similar methods.

Mindfulness Develops our Strength of Focus and Attention on the Moment

Untrained, our mind tends to slip from reflecting on the past or wondering about the future. It is often not really there in the present moment.

With practice and training in mindfulness we bring ourselves back to the raw reality of each moment, unadorned by daydreams, unencumbered by judgements. We notice just the actuality of a moment. What we actually see, clearly. What we hear, vibrantly. What we touch, sensitively. What we smell and what we taste.

Also what we are thinking or feeling emotionally.

We get better and better at this with practice. As we get better we start to enjoy things we previously ignored, and enjoy more vividly things we passively found pleasant.

In this way our positive experiences of life multiply and magnify, become a much bigger and richer part of the make up of our day. Every day.

Mindfulness Helps us Develop Great Mental Qualities in the Long-Term

The thousands of academic papers which demonstrate the many benefits of mindfulness can be summarised as follows. Developing our skills of mindfulness through frequent practice each day moves us increasingly in the direction of greater Clarity of thought, Calmness even under difficult situations, Contentment with life even when difficulties or painful experiences occur, and Compassion and Kindness towards others, not just humans, but everything that lives, including the planet as a whole.

We slowly increase a sense of deep love of life. Love of the mere reality of being alive. We learn to appreciate everyday things that we used to take for granted. That we get pure water from a tap. That we have a pillow on which to rest our head at night. And literally a thousand other things.

Mindfulness also develops in us a method and a habit which either lets go of, or deflects, negative states of mind or thoughts as and when they arise in our mind. This allows us to have less unhelpful experiences in our life and more positive ones.

How to do Mindfulness and Become More Mindful

There are two main ways in which to become better at being mindful.

The first is to simply try to notice more and more with our five senses and our mind. What do you see? What do you hear? At any given time.

Also what do you feel physically? This is about touch. But we misunderstand touch. We tend to think of it as only what we deliberately decide to touch, usually with our hands and fingers. But the fresh air touches your face and hands all the time you are outside. Air enters into your body through your nose and back out the same way or through your mouth, and you can feel its touch all the time. Your clothes touch your body so you can notice this at any time too. And you are always either standing, sitting or lying down, so your body is always in touch with something else; a chair, a floor or a pavement or road, or perhaps a pillow, a mattress and a duvet. Just notice all these things.

We also notice taste when we eat. This is a hugely important part of the enjoyment of eating but we often fail to fully absorb all those tastes. Likewise the final main sensation, smell. We have a lesser developed sense of smell than most animals but at times it can produce great pleasure or joy, the classic examples being the smell of coffee or fresh baking.

Notice that most of the things I have mentioned seem automatically quite pleasant. They are. This means with practice of pure noticing – i.e. mindfulness – we can actually experience literally hundreds of moments of pure immediate enjoyment every day, without doing anything different than we normally do. Just by walking, seeing, listening, noticing touch in all its forms, tasting food and drink, and smelling all that is pleasant.

The other main way of developing our ability to be mindful is through a more formal, exercise-like practice, usually called mindful meditation. I'm not a great fan of the word "meditation" as it brings to some people's minds images of mystical gurus, incense and bells, and a vague religious-spiritual connotation, which is attractive for some people but a bit off-putting for others. I prefer to just call it mindfulness practice.

The practice is simply a matter of finding a relatively quiet room or space where you can sit for anything between literally one minute or less up to as long as you want, with about ten to twenty minutes being most common.

You can do it lying down or sitting, and if sitting, you can do it on an ordinary chair, a couch, or a cushion. You can do it with feet on the floor as we'd normally sit, or cross-legged in the classic Hindu-Buddhist image of meditating. I sit on a kitchen chair because it is soft enough to be comfortable, hard enough to keep me alert, and its back is straight enough to keep me from slouching.

I prefer to close my eyes though you can do it eyes open, though there's more chance of distraction of course if your eyes are open.

I put one set of fingers on top of the other set, allow the thumbs to touch one another, and place my hands in that position onto the upper part of my lap. This keeps my hands from becoming fidgety while I practice. Then just do it for as long as you enjoy it. When you are ready to end a practice give yourself a minute or two to allow your eyes to very slowly and gently open so that you finish the practice with the same peaceful clarity of mind as you had during it.

Three Methods of Developing your Mind

Extinguishing: whenever a destructive or unhealthy mental state or idea or emotion arises; notice it; wait it out patiently until it fades away; or deflect it subtly by paying attention to your breath until the negative mental arising dies down. This is extinguishing negativities as they arise. It is like firefighting.

Preventing: in as much of your spare moments as possible practise deliberately noticing in a clear, calm, contented manner. Doesn't matter if it's clouds, sounds of a passing car, taste of a biscuit, anything is fine. The breath, or your feet on the ground are particularly easy and effective to do, with good results. These practices build up your mindfulness, and the corresponding clarity of thought, calmness of approach to life, and as these slowly build in you they help prevent the dominance of destructive mental states or creations.

Nurturing: when you can, try to deliberately cultivate compassion for others, and for all living things, by wishing everything that lives good fortune, security, safety, and enjoyment of life. Do the same with your own depth of appreciation and gratitude for all the everyday things we have that we usually take for granted. Together with breathing practice, which cultivates clarity of thought and calmness, these moment by moment practices can nurture the finest qualities we humans have, and do so, drop by drop in little moments over years and decades to come.

A Summary

1. Your life really matters. It is absolutely priceless.

2. It can only be lived in the present moment.

3. Therefore each moment is precious, and an opportunity, rich with potential.

4. Your mind is a problem and it is a gift.

5. The problem is it becomes automatic, habitual, and much of this is unhealthy for you.

6. Moreover your mind is poor at paying attention, and wanders from the present frequently.

7. Mindfulness, the skill of noticing clearly, helps deal with these problems of the mind.

8. It helps you become very familiar with how your mind works, so that you really know it well.

9. It helps you disarm or let go of unhelpful, negative things that your mind creates.

10. It helps you focus better on the present, which allows you to enjoy things more.

11. In the long-term it helps you become clearer, calmer, more content, and kinder.

12. Keep practising with everyday moments and with formal sitting practice.

13. Keep doing it! If you lapse don't worry or beat yourself up. Just get back to doing it.

14. Remember: Extinguish, Prevent, and Nurture as often as you can. Moment by moment.

Printed in Great Britain
by Amazon

SATURDAY NIGHT FOREVER
&
CYW

by **Roger Williams**

A Joio Publication
www.joio.co.uk
First published in 2016

A CIP catalogue record of this book is available from the British Library.

ISBN 978-0-9955215-0-6

Cover Design by Height Studio
Cover Photograph by Rhys Cozens
Typeset by Eira Fenn Gaunt, Caerdydd
Printed and bound in Wales

Roger Williams is an award-winning writer who has written plays for Theatr Genedlaethol Cymru (*Tir Sir Gâr*), Made in Wales (*Gulp & Killing Kangaroos*), Chapter (*Mother Tongue*), Theatr na nÓg (*Kapow!*), Sherman Cymru (*Surfing Carmarthen Bay*) and the Royal Welsh College of Music and Drama (*Y Byd [A'i Brawd]*).

He received the BAFTA Cymru screenwriter award for *Tir* (2015) and *Caerdydd* (2010) and created the Celtic Media Festival award-winning drama series *Gwaith/Cartref* for S4C. His drama series *Tales from Pleasure Beach* for BBC2 was BAFTA nominated and he has written for a number of long-running television dramas including *The Story of Tracy Beaker* and *Hollyoaks*.

Mae'r dramodydd Roger Williams wedi ysgrifennu dramâu ar gyfer nifer o gwmnïau theatr gan gynnwys Theatr Genedlaethol Cymru (*Tir Sir Gâr*), Made in Wales (*Gulp & Killing Kangaroos*), Chapter (*Mother Tongue*), Theatr na nÓg (*Kapow!*), Sherman Cymru (*Surfing Carmarthen Bay*) a Choleg Brenhinol Cerdd a Drama Cymru (*Y Byd [A'i Brawd]*).

Derbyniodd Roger y wobr am yr awdur gorau yng ngwobrau BAFTA Cymru am *Tir* (2015) a *Caerdydd* (2010) a fe greodd y gyfres *Gwaith/Cartref* a enillodd wobr yr Ŵyl Cyfryngau Celtaidd. Enwebwyd ei gyfres *Tales from Pleasure Beach* ar gyfer BBC2 am wobr BAFTA ac mae ef wedi ysgrifennu sgriptiau ar gyfer cyfresi teledu eraill gan gynnwys *The Story of Tracy Beaker* a *Hollyoaks*.

SATURDAY NIGHT FOREVER

by **Roger Williams**

First produced in 1998 by CF1.theatre.com at Chapter Arts Centre, Cardiff and on tour:

Lee – Sean Carlsen
Director – Steven Fisher
Designer – Carolyn Willits
Lighting designer – Simon Wheatley

A second major production was staged by the Sherman Theatre, Cardiff in 2001:

Lee – Darren Lawrence
Director – Steven Fisher
Designer – Ellen Woods

This version of the text was first produced by Aberystwyth Arts Centre & Joio at Aberystwyth Arts Centre and on tour in November 2015:

Lee – Delme Thomas
Director – Kate Wasserberg
Designer – Zakk Hein
Sound designers – Talbott/Ashfield
Stage Manager – Bethan Dawson
Producer – Gareth Roberts

LEE

LEE, a man in his mid-20s, addresses the audience.

Saturday night started at one o'clock. At least that's when it started for Matthew. One o'clock, Saturday afternoon.

You'd be lucky to get a word out of him before he'd checked Facebook and Tweeted. With statuses commented on and pictures liked, Matthew'd yawn wide, prize himself from the memory foam and announce, 'I'm going to get ready. Five minutes alright?'

And an hour later he'd be back. Appearing at the top of the stairs like a Strictly contestant primed to take to the floor. Preened, moisturised... he'd waltz towards the door... check his Visa card and fringe were safely in place before pulling on a jacket. Saturday night was coming and, in order to make the most of it, Matthew had to prepare.

You see, in Matthew's world, Saturday nights were important. Too important to pass by without some kind of celebration or event. Saturday nights like days off, freebies and salted caramel chocolates were meant to be enjoyed. Saturday nights were to be treasured, valued. He counted the days go by each week like an excited child working his way through an advent calendar.

Matthew loved the ritual of dressing up and going out. Drinking, laughing and dancing until the DJ's head was ready to hit the pillow. It was his religion and, like other true believers, Matthew gave it everything. After all, Saturday nights only came round once a week and you had to make the most of them. Procedures had to be followed, questions asked and decisions made. Where? When? And probably most importantly: 'What on earth am I going to wear?'

1

The first two questions were easily answered with a quick text to a fellow worshipper. 'Golden Cross, half-eight.' But the other problem was more of a challenge. And after rifling through an overworked wardrobe that was near to bursting, he'd give up, and decide emergency action had to be taken. In other words – he needed to go shopping.

Matthew was a pro, and would willingly spend all Saturday searching the rails for something new to wear. H&M, All Saints... dodging mums with sprogs in a dash across the Hayes to TK Maxx. He searched for something loud and different. Something garish, or see-through, that could only ever be worn in the shadows of a night-club, where the fashion police weren't on patrol and everyone else was too high to care. He wanted a clubber's uniform; something that said to everyone else in the room, 'Hey! Look at me! I'm having a fabulous time, and I'm wearing the top to prove it!'

Matthew was scrupulous in his selection. And it was only when he had found something special, and believe me, he would always find something special, that he'd relax and agree to go home. Chuffed to bits, he'd sit on the back seat of the bus grinning gormlessly like a big kid; satisfied, complete. In a world of his own, he'd be privately mixing and matching every pair of trousers he already owned with the shirt he'd just bought. Saturday night was coming and he was planning his look. 'Tonight's going to be awesome,' he'd whisper, before deciding whether he wanted fish-fingers or spaghetti for tea.

Surrounded by his new purchases he'd collapse in front of the television and publish his plans for the night to his one thousand and eighty nine Facebook friends. 'Longest week ever. Can't wait to get steaming tonight. LOL.' Lazing contentedly amongst a sea of carrier bags, he'd ride a wave of reaction to his status while Keith Lemon rubbed himself up against a member of The Saturdays in the background.

As Matthew scrolled through Amy Hall's pics of a girl's away-day to Bristol and admired Olly Murr's bum on the X-Factor, he prayed the night ahead would go to plan. Only when Cheryl Fernandez-Versini had told the checkout girl from Wigan that she'd 'smashed it one-hundred-and-ten-percent' would Matthew stir and start to get ready.

Every so often he'd appear semi-dressed and panic-stricken with a mouthful of questions. 'Is this shirt too tight? Do these trousers make my arse look big? What'll I do with my hair?' And I'd give answers that were always ignored because, not answering to the name of Stella McCartney, I obviously didn't know what the hell I was talking about. 'Yes, too tight.' 'What arse?' and 'Oh, just cut it all off!'

Miraculously, as the cab was pulling up outside, he'd saunter into the hall on cue with every single hair on his head suffocated in a layer of product. The shirt he'd bought earlier that afternoon gripped to his freshly-shaven chest like cling-film. 'Right,' he'd declare, 'Ready. And I'll tell you something for nothing, I'm going to get wasted tonight.'

A few drinks here-and-there later – Peppermint, Wow – Matthew'd inevitably make his final pilgrimage to the same old club, where he'd have one drink too many and motor around the dance floor like a wind-up toy. He'd wail along to Taylor Swift, strut to Rita Ora, and stand still, cross-armed, refusing to dance another step in protest, when the DJ dared to play anything that fell below ninety beats per minute.

Matthew loved Saturday night, and I hated him for it. I hated the way he gossiped with his pack of friends at the bar, flirted with strangers, and drank WKD suggestively from its bottle. Always the same game. I could guarantee that by the end of the night, he'd be pig drunk, would've snorted speed with the enthusiasm of a hand-held Dyson, and jumped up on stage to mime the part of Perrie when the DJ played Black Magic.

So it was, to say the least then, a bit of a problem that Matthew was my boyfriend, and that we'd been seeing each other for three months.

Matthew and I were a match made in Grindr. I'd downloaded the app to my 'phone for the thousandth time – and despite the time-wasters, liars, married men – I was willing to give it another go. I was looking for love. And if my ideal man wasn't available, a quick wank wouldn't go amiss.

The app revealed scores of men like me who'd posted a profile in the hope of finding a partner – for life, the night or just five minutes round the back of Asda.

Profile names were carefully crafted: 'Horny hung guy.' 'Bottom 4 top.' 'Cock Now.' Grindr – where failed copywriters went to die. 'No pic, no reply.' 'Everything but anal.' 'Put my dog down today, need cheering up.'

Everyone exaggerated the truth a little. Men who were 5'10" were elevated to 6 foot. Average bodies became 'toned'. Everyone joined a tribe. Bears, twinks, daddies, jocks... All looking for chat, friends, relationships... but ultimately admitting they were also interested in 'no strings'. Discreet – or more often than not – 'discret', fun.

The images mostly showed men with their tops off or men in their pants. Super soft porn. The unashamed showed their faces, others were anonymous. Also added to the mix was the random image of a dog or a dolphin. And occasionally the very random image of a man in a gas mask.

Knowing that first impressions count, I chose my profile pic carefully. I spent ages trying to take a decent picture of myself on my phone in front of the bathroom mirror. Belly in, chest out, smile, click... I gave up, convinced I looked more like Moe from the Simpsons than the kind of guy you'd take home to meet your mother. Eventually I found a photo of myself on a beach holiday. Tanned, thin, looking a bit buff... Phwoah, I would.

I edited the colours – Nashville Filter – cropped it to within an inch of its digital life until all you could see of my photoshopped body was the bit from my neck to my knees – and posted it.

Seconds later came the first response. 'Hey! What you up to?' The second, 'Hot bod, mate.' The third, 'What U into?' I entered into dialogues that clearly weren't going anywhere and then up popped Matthew with the opening line: 'Nice teeth'. I laughed out loud.

We met for a drink that turned into a night at his place. He wasn't my usual type but he was a pastry chef and gave really good blow-jobs. It was a combination of talents any man would have trouble saying no to.

It was fun, for a while. But the truth I couldn't escape was that Matthew and I were fundamentally different. I was a custard slice and he was a Belgian bun. I stargazed while he howled at the moon. Matthew hit the dance-floor looking for laughs, I took up a defensive position at the bar.

For the record, I didn't dance. I just don't. I'm one of those people you see in night clubs standing at the edge of the dance-floor watching everyone else let go. One of those people you find looking on. Allergic to rhythm.

I make an effort of course. I mouth the lyrics like a goldfish, tap my foot to the beat, and sway back and forth just to show willing. A spectator at a football match I'll never be good enough to play in. I wasn't Premier League like Matthew.

Nobody in my family can dance. It's hereditary. Like the colour of your eyes or the size of your feet. At the school disco in 1998 I found out the hard way the dreaded gene had been passed on to me. As the Spice Girls's *Spice Up Your Life* bled from the sound system, I died on the dance-floor surrounded by my so-called mates. Shot down by the laughter of every boy and every girl on the school roll, I quickly accepted that some people simply weren't built to dance. And after Cerian Jones's public admonishment that I was 'An embarrassment!' who, 'Should've stayed at home with the rest of the saddos!' I gave up, and learnt to deliver a firm 'no' when anyone suggested heading towards the flashing lights.

I discovered mountains of excuses as I trekked from party to pub, and disco to night-club, en route through the landscape of a Saturday night. 'Can't dance sorry, twisted my ankle playing rugby last night, and it really hurts, ow.' 'Dying for a piss. You go ahead, I'll catch you up.' Like Doctor David Banner I'd lurk in the shadows. 'Don't make me dance. You really wouldn't like me when I dance.'

So when Saturday night came round and we headed into town, I clung to the edge of the pool while everyone else splashed about in the deep end.

'So? You gonna dance with us tonight then mister or what?' Matthew asked when he was bored of playing with his new friends. The 'D' word. 'Alright. Don't be so touchy. It's not like anyone's looking at you is it?'

Perhaps I should've kept my mouth shut. Perhaps I should've bitten my lip and ended the relationship if not gracefully, then at least sober. But I didn't. And instead, I snapped. As I watched Matthew revelling with his disciples under the blazing lights and buzz of the room I said it, and in doing so, broke his faith.

It was when a Take That megamix exploded from the speakers that it happened. Usually I wouldn't've minded, but having already endured Justin Bieber and One Direction, I'd had enough. As soon as I heard Gary Barlow's deafening warble I could feel it building up inside me. The rage. The anger. The hatred against a playlist that needed burning.

No way back. Pushed off the ledge and falling faster than a body builder from a tenth floor window, I found myself turning to Matthew, just turning to him and saying, 'Take That are shit.'
'You what?' he asked, not quite hearing me I don't think over the music and cries of ecstasy that were flying up from the crowd.
'Take That are shit. I hate Take That.'
'Don't be a wanker, Lee. They're classic,' Matthew replied, gulping at his cider, and waving over his approval to a DJ who loved to throw in the occasional ironic hit and watch the crowd wallow in nostalgia.
'Well, I do. I really hate them.'
'No you don't.'
'I do! I wish the other three had fucked off into obscurity with Jason Orange too.'

And it was that comment that did it. He looked at me as if I'd plunged a knife deep into his chest, 'But, but, we like Take That.'
'No Matthew, you like Take That. You like Take That, the same as you like TOWIE, Candy Crush, ready-mixed Mojitos, and this fucking hole. I don't. I never have done.'

'Bollocks,' he responded.
'Yeah. It is isn't it?'

I left before his tears could dry.

LEE

LEE undoes the top button of his shirt and rolls up his sleeves.

Saturday nights 'in' were a cause to be championed. Once I would've been trekking up Mill Lane at nine o'clock on a Saturday night, but now I was holed up at home in a pair of old jogging bottoms trying to decipher the plot of *Doctor Who*. I took Saturday nights off. I didn't shave, didn't dress up, didn't have to make small talk over loud music in confined spaces. This was life after Matthew. Bliss.

But like a new pair of trainers, the novelty soon wore off. Like life without WiFi or a vegetarian diet, self-imposed exile had drawbacks. I was missing the terrain of the social circuit. I worried I was missing out on something. This was the fifth Saturday in succession I'd spent at home watching *In It to Win It* with my hands down the front of my jogging bottoms. I couldn't carry on like this! So when I heard that Emma from the office was having a party at the weekend I ended my Saturday sabbatical and grabbed the invite as a lifeline. 'When d'you want me?'

Saturday came round and I ventured outside again with a bottle of Smirnoff wedged under my arm and headed over to Riverside for salvation. It was dark. I'd forgotten what it was like to be out at this time on a weekend. Groups of friends on the way to the pub pushed past me pumped up for another big Saturday adventure. Excited. Primed. Men on a mission lumbered by with great expectations and even bigger imaginations.

'Hardly any point me goin' out tonight, boys. Wait an' see, I'll be back home again by nine doing the business with some lucky young lady on the bedroom carpet.'
'Nine o'clock? Slow worker aren't you?'

'And I'll leave her in no doubt that heaven, contrary to popular opinion, is a place on earth.'
'Yeah, but I don't think anyone'll believe it's in Ely.'

And as they moved by laughing in their scoop neck T-shirts revealing tattoos on bulging biceps, I felt a little uneasy, scared. The geography was unfamiliar, foreign, and standing here as a stranger it struck me as volatile, unsafe.

Beauty queens in training were doing their bit for girl power in Max Factor colours and halter neck tops on Romilly Road. Wrapped up in small dresses that'd look 'Stunnin'!' under the lights, they bared the cold wind in a mist of hair-spray and came out together for fun.
'Lindsey! Lindsey! Are you comin' or what? It's half-past eight already an' I said we'd be there by quarter past! Never mind yer zits girl, with them puppies on show they're not gonna be looking at yer face!'
An animal out of hibernation, my senses heightened. I waited for something to explode, for one of the lairy passers-by to approach me, stop me, jeer at me.
'We goin' down Revolution, Jude? I loves it there.'
The stuff of dreams.

A car sped past me, its stereo growling, and the paranoia won over.
'Keep your head down. Low profile. Don't provoke anyone. You're alright. Keep walking. Keep moving.'

The party was well under way by the time I arrived. Emma greeted me at the door, draped herself around my neck like a feather boa, and pinched my bum.
'Alright beautiful?' she croaked.
They'd been drinking since lunchtime and I could feel the haze of alcohol rising on her breath like steam from a boiling hot bath.

'Hey Paula, this is the one I was telling you about!'
Paula, Emma's best mate, was wrapped up in some strange man's arms talking horoscopes and admiring his deltoids.
'The agoraphobic? Bless. Quite cute isn't he?'
'Don't start getting ideas, mind. He doesn't travel on our bus.'
'Got a car have he?'
'No, stupid. He likes cock.'

Alright, perhaps I am exaggerating, but I could've sworn that at that moment every head in the room turned one hundred and eighty degrees and looked at me. Freeze frame. The monkey boy. The man with three nipples.

'Lush to see you babes,' Emma wailed. 'I'll be back in a sec. Just got to go and strangle whoever's playing this music. Shit, isn't it?' With which she fled in search of whoever'd hijacked Spotify and was playing the soundtrack from *Glee*.

I struggled to find a familiar face, someone I could latch onto. No joy. Watching so many socially adept people at work only made me feel like even more of an outsider. I didn't speak this language. Like a resident of Port Talbot lost in Caernarfon, I didn't understand. 'You what?' I felt self-conscious, I wanted Emma to come back and translate. The paranoia was kicking in. Norman- no-mates. Stranger in the corner. I considered the options. Go. Stay. Leave. Dissolve...

'You're Lee, aren't you? Carl. Emma's brother. I hate going to parties where I don't know anyone.'
A fellow traveller.
'You too? I'm glad I'm not the only one who feels like a total dick.'
'Well, no. I know most of the people here. I mean you. Emma said you haven't been going out that much lately.'
Could Emma have a bigger mouth?

'Bad break up was it?'

Yes, she could.

'I've been through something similar myself recently. Two years we were together.'

'Ah, right.'

The conversation lumbered to a halt. I couldn't think of anything sensible to say so I didn't. The music stopped. Emma must've won her battle with the DJ. I shuffled uncomfortably in my chair, trying to think of a way to jump-start the conversation that wouldn't have sounded naff. Carl beat me to it. And taking my glass from my hand asked, 'Top up?'

And with that single shot of vodka the conversation took off and veered wildly from subject to subject like an out-of-control car being driven by a twelve-year-old. Everyone else in the house danced, copped off, and got high, while Carl and I had great discussions about everything that's important in life. Politics, culture, *The Big Bang Theory*...

Look, I know I promised myself it wouldn't happen again. I know I'd sworn that I wasn't going to, under any circumstances, go back to that place, that nightmare place I'd just escaped from, but, as we talked, and as I laughed, I think that for the first time since breaking up with Matthew, I actually started to fancy somebody.

Carl was a teacher. Carl came from Penarth. Carl had a degree in Sociology. Carl drank lager. Carl had gone to Copenhagen on his holidays. Carl was gorgeous and I would've joined his fan club right there and then if he'd had one. He was tall, with cropped black hair, and a chiselled face that could've sold suits for Armani. So what was the problem? The problem was, as Carl told me at precisely four-thirty-three in the morning and after far too much booze, that he'd just split up with Debbie.

Ok, so I might've known deep down that my chances of getting past first base with this man were slim, but you've got to have hope haven't you? And the longer we'd talked the further I'd fallen, but the mention of Debbie crushed the castle I'd been building. He'd had a girlfriend. He was straight. He couldn't help it.

It was late and this last blow was too much. Carl was a nice man. We'd had a great conversation during which I'd deluded myself we would've made a great couple. Somewhere in my fantasy world I'd even picked out a colour scheme for our living room. Ice grey if you must know, feature wall Saphire. But I didn't particularly want to sit around super gluing his broken ego back together. Especially since the incentive of a snog had been cruelly snatched away from me. Carl was getting over a failed relationship. It was Sunday morning. Very early Sunday morning. I wanted a wee. I wanted to go home. What I didn't want to hear about was Debbie. So before he could go any further, I made an executive decision, stood up, and left.

As I stepped out onto a deserted Rolls Street I was bitten by the cold wind. I stuffed my hands down deep into my pockets and hunched myself up tight. 'Bloody heterosexuals. They get every-where.' I hadn't gone far before Carl caught up with me.
'Hey, why d'you dash off like that? Did I say something wrong?'
'No, I'm just tired.'
'We were getting on well weren't we? I thought you liked me.'
The white noise faded. Normal service resumed.
'Debbie broke up with me, because…' I could feel my heart beat-ing. 'Because…' Faster.
What?
'Because I finally plucked up to the courage,' he waited, bit his lip, '…to tell her I liked men. I mean, that I'm, y'know... gay, like.'

As impossible as it seems now, this beautiful man I'd been chasing around inside my head all night had just come out to me. Standing in the middle of the street, barefoot, at something-hideous-past-four in the morning, this seemingly straight, football playing, lager drinker, who looked a bit like Henry Cavill, had come out to me.

Carl stared wide-eyed, puzzled, waiting for a reaction other than shock to cross my face. There was a gap where language froze in the cold morning air, and it seemed only right that at that surreal moment fireworks should've gone off somewhere, that great big rockets should've screamed across the sky and burst open. Flashes of red, yellow, green. An orchestra should've started playing and Carl's family come running out of the surrounding houses to embrace him like a game-show winner, congratulated him for having the guts to tell the world, well, me at least, that he was gay. It didn't happen of course. It never does.

Carl looked down at his feet and waited for an answer. He shivered. I desperately wanted to say something that would make it all better, make him feel alright. Say something clever and profound that'd put all his fears to rest. But all I could say at that particular moment was, 'Chilly, isn't it?' And he agreed that it was.

LEE

LEE undoes another couple of buttons on his shirt.

We didn't do it that night of course. We didn't! I mean, I didn't kiss him. Nor did I drag him back to my place, strip him naked, and throw myself at him like a wet tea towel at a chip pan fire. No, I waited until the following weekend before I did that.

As I walked along Cathedral Road to keep the date we'd made my brain went into panic. Would Carl turn out to be Matthew mark two? Was there a disco queen lurking beneath his mild mannered exterior? He was too good to be true... What if he was a serial killer, or a UKIP supporter? But as I neared the pub and saw Carl standing waiting for me wearing a battered pair of jeans, trainers, and one of those hooded tops zipped half way up I knew I was doing the right thing. His hair was its usual scruffy self and when he saw me coming he raised a hand, sniffed and said, 'Alright?' From the size of the smile on my face I think he knew that it was.

Carl wasn't like Matthew. Carl listened. He wasn't hyperactive. Carl read the newspaper, and could sit through an entire film at the cinema without getting up to fetch popcorn. Carl didn't talk all the way through a good TV programme, didn't spend hours in front of a mirror, liked mountain bikes, walking and thought One Direction should've been drowned at birth. Let's just say we had things in common.

We walked slowly away from the pub after last orders and headed down Llandaff Road. The streets of Cardiff were sleeping, but as we turned the corner we very nearly walked into the middle of a fight. A sudden nightmare. Two men throwing punches. Shouting and swearing like nobody's business. Danger. One of them dropped his chips. 'Bastard! My curry sauce!' Carl reassuringly put an arm around my shoulder and steered me away.

'Here we are then.'
'Yeah, here we are.'
We were standing under a street light outside my flat. I hunted for my door key. Carl waited. He wasn't going anywhere. Imagine a hideous pause as we watched one another trying to act casual under the lamp's hazy Western Power glow. Both freezing. Both longing to go inside. But both waiting for the other to suggest it first.
'Live here alone then, d'you?'
Opening question. Let's get the ball rolling.
'With a couple of friends yeah.'
Friendly smile, casual response.
'It looks nice.'
And that was the comment I'd been waiting for which allowed me to go one stage further. I acted as though a sudden brain wave had just hit me, and spontaneously asked, 'Oh, well, do you want to come in and have a look round?' So alright, it wasn't that much further up the evolutionary scale than, 'Quick coffee?' but it did the job, and after a quick tour of the house we sat in the lounge, still talking, still eyeing each other up. Horny teenagers on a school trip.

I sat back casually on the sofa, took a deep breath, and turned to face him. Now in my experience there's a point in these situations when you've got to stop the chit-chat and get down to business. A moment when you've got to do nothing except look at the person you're gagging for very late at night, blatantly stare at them until they get the message. It then becomes pretty difficult for the other person to ignore the fact that what you really want to do is stop the mindless conversation and snog.

So I kept looking at Carl. Watching his mouth motoring away. Studying his face. The object of the mission must be to make eye contact, hold it, wait until that precious moment when your head's buzzing because you know the inevitable is just around the corner, seize the opportunity, hold your nerve, lean forward, and swoop in for the kill. Making certain of course that lips are fully locked.

'Tonight's been a laugh, hasn't it?'
'Yeah, it's been good,' I replied, giving him a playful punch on his thigh, and then skilfully resting the flat of my hand on his leg. Good tactic that one. Moment of truth.

Carl looked at my hand.
'Emma said this would happen.'
'What?' I asked, trying not to think about my heart that was thumping so hard by now he must've been able to hear it.
'This.' And that's when he leaned over, met me halfway, and we kissed.

His lips touched mine. Hovered for a second, then touched again. He pulled away a fraction, smiled, then drove forward again to kiss me. His stubble brushed my face, and I could feel his breath burning fast and warm on my neck.

In the semi-darkness of my bedroom, he lifted his shirt over his head. He was hairy. Not Planet of the Apes hairy. He wasn't Tom Selleck's twin. But he had enough of a layer for nobody to be in any doubt he was producing testosterone for Wales.

I traced my hand down towards his belly button and unbuckled his belt. He stepped out of his trousers and stood before me in his pants and socks, waiting. I looked him up and down, admiring his package that was getting bigger by the second. Trust me, Carl had nothing to be worried about. Yet he seemed anxious,vulner-able. I did the only thing I could do, and took advantage of him.

LEE

My friends were sick to death of hearing about Carl. 'Oh, it's all Carl these days isn't it? Carl, Carl, Carl. You're Carl mad, mun.' They said he was an unhealthy obsession that would end with me in tears on a rooftop somewhere threatening to jump. But they were only jealous. Like I said – everyone liked Carl. You couldn't help it.

We'd been seeing each other for six-months by now, a sort of anniversary, and Carl wanted to celebrate.
'We should go out.'
'Out?'
'Yeah, well we can't stay in on such a special night. I reckon we should do something.'
'Like what?'
'I don't know. Go to a club or something.'

Club? Club? That'd mean… The 'D' word. Somewhere in the back of my mind I was still having nightmares where I could clearly picture Matthew, jigging up and down to Beyonce and gasping on an e-cigarette with his friends by the DJ booth. I even wondered if I would bump into him. After all, Cardiff city centre on a Saturday was Matthew's stamping ground. I worried what'd happen if our eyes met across a smoky bar, and planned what I'd say to him in case sodium did meet water. I chickened out. Let's face it, after my experience with Matthew, a Bake Off hopeful had more chance of getting a souffle to rise in a cool oven than Carl had of getting me into a club.

'Trust me, I won't make you dance. Honest.'
I looked him in the eye. And believed him.
'Ok. But I'm not going out with you looking like that, you'll have to get changed.'

He was just about to complain when I said, 'Fair's fair, Carl.'
He pulled himself up from the sofa, sighed, and turned to leave the room.
'I'm going to get ready. Five minutes, alright?'

And five minutes later, he was ready.
'Come on. It's Saturday night. We're young, free, and alright, we're not single, but we are living in the closest capital city to London.' He always said that. A walking billboard for Visit Wales.
'Let's go out and make the most of it, yeah?'
I switched off the light and followed him through the door.
Another Saturday night in Cardiff.

Sitting in the wine bar on St. Mary's Street we lost track of time and exactly how many units of alcohol our brain cells were absorbing. The place was packed with swaying Cardiffians out for a ball and the live entertainment that was advertised on every available inch of wall.

It was well after I'd started slurring that Lorraine came to the stage and blew hard into her microphone. 'Oh good, it's turned on,' she grinned. 'An' it's not the only thing on this stage tonight that's turned on either!'

Lorraine was a vision in denim. Her hair bleached blonde so many times even her roots had forgotten their original colour. Carl returned from the bar with another round and I leapt hungrily at the bag of cheese and onion crisps he was, by now, trained to automatically get.
'You've been a long time!'
'There was a queue!' And he grinned.

Lorraine piped up again. 'Now 'en boys an' girls. As you know, Saturday night's entertainment night…' A loud cheer went up. 'Frisky lot tonight, aren't you?' Lorraine came alive on nights like tonight. The centre of attention. 'Well you're not going to be disappointed. Because it's that time of the month again... Watch it! The time of the month for karaoke!'

And with that word the drunk element of the crowd jumped for joy while the sober element reached for their coats. I was somewhere in the middle. Jumping and reaching. 'An' startin' us off tonight...' The smile on Carl's face was growing. 'A brave young soul...' Getting wider and... No way. 'A cute little thing I'm told too...' I knew what was coming next. 'So give the lad a welcome...' No escape. 'Give a big round of applause to...' It was too late. 'Lee from Cardiff!'

The crowd barked like wild dogs, delighted not to be the first victim. 'Come on, Lee. Don't be shy now,' Lorraine ordered. Carl pulled me to my feet, and I had a sudden urge to go bungee-jumping, swimming in shark infested waters, dancing... anything but, anything, but, sing!

I'd been set up. Carl, evil boyfriend, had set me up. And as Lorraine dragged me kicking and screaming to the stage, I looked back and promised revenge.

That stage, right then, was the loneliest place in the world. I was standing there alone, with nothing but a microphone for company, pissed-up, drunk and in possession of a dangerous weapon – my voice.

'Is everyone ready?' I closed my eyes. Reminded myself the ordeal would be over in three minutes. Three minutes and I'd be sitting down again. Three minutes and Carl, who was standing on his chair now – whooping – would be dumped, three minutes... The music kicked in. I realised I didn't even know what song I was supposed to be singing. What had Carl chosen for me? Fuck! What was I meant to...

We hear Take That's 'Greatest Day' in karaoke style.

No. Anything but this… Please, anything but… Deep breaths, don't panic, don't spew –

LEE begins to sing the track. Nervous at first but growing in confidence to a triumphant finish.

Back at the table, I downed the drink that was waiting for me in one gulp.
'Oh, come on Adele! You must see the funny side?'
Funny, my arse.
'It was a surprise! An anniversary surprise!'
'Surprise? I'd have preferred a surprise like this…'
And it was then that I pulled a small package wrapped in silver paper from my pocket and dropped it onto the table.
'You're not about to ask me to marry you are you.'
'Just open it, Carl.'
He undid the paper carefully and lifted up the lid.
'It's beautiful.'
With which he reached over the table and gripped my hand. His new watch shining under the mirror-ball.

We walked up towards the castle in a dream. They'd already hung the Christmas lights and the street was littered with people heading off to clubs. A bunch of students were arguing with a cab driver outside Howells. A man in a bright yellow shirt was chucking up in front of Pizza Express. We kept walking.

I don't remember crossing the road or what we talked about, but as we approached Sophia Gardens Carl ran on ahead of me. Playing, I ran after him down the path, into the park, and finally caught up with him by one of the tall trees that line the long road up towards the Swalec stadium. He was out of breath, exhilarated. He leaned up against the trunk of a tree.

'I've loved tonight, I've loved the bar, I've loved the entertainment.'
He paused to catch his breath. 'I love my watch, and I love…'
He hesitated, playing the game we normally played with one another.

'What?' I was supposed to ask. And he would normally reply 'Tom Hardy', but tonight he didn't, tonight he was being serious, tonight he said: 'And I love, you.'

It was cold. There were a few clouds in the sky, but not nearly enough to obscure the handful of stars that were still up.

'I do. I love you.'

He kissed me.

'I know,' I told him. I looked him in the eye, and everything was alright.

'And if you wanted to ask me to marry you, I'd probably say yes.'

'Probably?'

'Marriage, dog, kids… Comes to everyone eventually.'

Hand in hand, we headed home.

His hand was the first thing I lost. It's funny because I can still remember exactly what it felt like. Soft, warm, safe. But that night, when we were ripped apart, his hand was the first thing I lost. No more dream. Someone spat, kicked. I remembered trying to get up. But scrambling to my feet was useless and I was swept back down to the floor in one move, hard.

'Watch the bender squirm.'

The attackers were laughing and soon there were two men bearing down on me. Punching. Kicking. Grinding their fists into my body. I could hear Carl further along the road shouting, but couldn't make out exactly what he was saying over the jeers of the men. They were shouting so loud, so loud I was sure someone would hear.

'Fancy yourself do you queer? Fancy a bit do you? Go on lads. Give the fucking queer what he fucking deserves.'

I tried to kick. But like the tiny kid getting a hiding on the school yard I was useless. Like the old man attacked in his own front room where he watches TV, I wasn't strong enough. Like the young girl cornered thirty seconds away from her own front door, I couldn't call for help. There were too many. Their punches rained down on top of me. Hail stones on tarmac.

Someone grabbed a fistful of hair and knocked my head against the ground like a drum. Crack. Crack. A foot struck my stomach, and forced the air from out of me. I wanted to be sick.

The beating stopped. I thought it was over. Innocently prayed they might now let me go. I ached for a second before feeling someone tugging at my clothes. 'No, please, no, don't,' I begged, and looked up again to try and find a human face.
'This'll show the dirty queer. This'll finish it.'

I tried to stop them ripping away my shirt, tried to stop them mauling me, tried to get up and run. Run! The blade pressed into my flesh. 'No, no, don't.' I could feel myself bleeding. Sharp, cold, clean. I knew I was bleeding. 'Please, no.' I looked up again, but all I could see was the shining blade of a Stanley knife coming down for seconds. 'Fuck! No!' Again. Again. The blade tore my skin. Again.
'Get him lower,' someone screamed.
I wriggled, begged them 'No!' But the blade came down again, lower, lower, again lower, and as they slashed at my groin with the knife, I passed out.

Lee undoes the final few buttons on his shirt and shows his scars.

LEE

They've healed. They said all along they would. That they'd get better.

Mum was watching day-time telly when I woke up, chewing on a toffee, and holding my hand. I opened my eyes and watched the TV too for a while, until Mum turned round to unwrap another sweet and saw that I was conscious. She looked at me, tried to say something, but couldn't, and instead, she cried. Dad was just outside. He's never liked hospitals. Always has to leave the room to escape the stench of disinfectant. But he came back in when my mum called. I didn't cry. Not then. I didn't cry until later.

Lee begins to dress.

They stayed all day that day. They were trying to look after me like they had when I was little and home from school with mumps or measles. Dad brought me a pile of magazines. But they weren't the copies of *Smash Hits* he'd brought home for me when I was still his little boy. He'd chosen more carefully now. *GQ, Attitude, What Car?* There was a carrier bag of sweets and fruit. A bottle of Coke, and a bundle of new clothes, socks, underwear, bought two days earlier from Marks and Spencer and folded neatly inside my bedside locker. They took care of me. They wanted to. But this wasn't chicken pox. And they knew it.

I'd been beaten, kicked, cut, and my parents, had to face me like this, with the bruises and scars on full show, reminding them every time they looked at me what'd happened. And I had to face them. That was the hardest part. I mean, what are you supposed to say to your Mum and Dad when you've been thrashed for being a dirty little queer? When a complete stranger has taken a blade to your balls and cut you, because he didn't like what he saw one night.

It wasn't easy. Embarrassing. Difficult. But not easy. Especially for Mum, who was left to tell me that Carl was also attacked, also beaten, but hadn't been so lucky. How was she meant to explain that he wouldn't be coming through the door with a silly big grin slapped across his face any minute now? Because one Saturday night, one stupid Saturday night, a group of lads got together, had a few cans, and decided to have a laugh.

Dad talked to the police every morning who said they would be pressing for a conviction, but as yet didn't have any definite leads. But they were trying. They told me it was a good thing I hadn't had the chance to go home, shower, change my clothes. There'd be more evidence this way. But why hadn't I stayed on the main road? Why didn't I stay where there were other people who could've seen, could've done something to help? I should've made more noise, I should've got a better view of the attackers, I should've taken a taxi, I should've stayed home, I should've…

I asked Dad to ask them for Carl's watch. I wanted to keep it. Wear it. He came back the next day, and told me they hadn't found a watch. Was it meant to be reported stolen?

A week later, when Mum and Dad decided I could probably be left alone for a few hours, I heard a familiar voice in the corridor. A head popped round the door.

'Ooh-lah-lah! Private room? Very swish.'

It was Matthew.

'Now, I've brought you everything you'll need. Moisturiser: we don't want to go sacrificing our good looks now do we? The air-conditioning in these places dries your skin out something terrible. My iPad – I downloaded a couple of those foreign detective thingies you like – don't ask me what, it's all Dutch to me. And a box of Ferrero Rocher. But don't go eating them all at once otherwise you'll put on even more weight, and I don't want to be held responsible for that.'

He danced around the room, joking and laughing before finally crash landing on the edge of my bed.
'Ooh. Quite comfy isn't it?'
He smiled.
'Well? How's the patient?'

And that's when I cried.

So, Matthew hugged me, and stayed until I stopped.

Lee considers the microphone at the side of the stage. He walks towards it and reprises Take That's 'Greatest Day'. But this time it's haunting and poignant.

Blackout.

CYW

gan **Roger Williams**

Perfformiwyd *Cyw* am y tro cyntaf yng nghanolfan y celfyddydau Chapter fel rhan o ŵyl Queer Cymru ym mis Awst 2007. Ysgrifennwyd y ddrama wedi ymosodiadau ar y gymuned hoyw yn Moscow y flwyddyn honno.

Cyw – Ryan Chappell
Cyfarwyddwr – Roger Williams

RHAN I

O ffenest 'yn 'stafell wely ar y degfed llawr o'n i'n gallu gweld pethe rhyfeddol. Cestyll ysblennydd, brogaod ffyrnig, a thywysogion golygus yn hela llygod mawr, enfawr. 'Y nghyfrinach i oedd yr olygfa hon. 'Y ngolygfa i.

Dim ond unwaith wnes i fentro rhannu gydag unrhyw un 'yn fersiwn i o beth o'dd tu hwnt i'r gwydr. Gwennodd 'yn fam ar ôl i fi ddisgrifio'r bwrlwm llachar. Y cwbwl yr o'dd hi'n gallu 'i weld o'dd blocie a blocie o fflatie… 'Tria 'to!' …dynion ar eu ffordd adre o'r ffatri… ''Drycha!' …plant drygionus yn crwydro'r strydoedd… 'Plis!' …a char heddlu yn cadw llygad barcud ar y bobol bach.

'Mae 'da dy fab ddychymyg bywiog iawn, Mrs. Gabuzov,' wedodd 'yn athrawes wrth Mam un diwrnod.

Oes, Hen Wrach. Bywiog iawn.

* * *

Bydde'r ffatri'n cau bob haf am bythefnos a bydde Mam a finne'n gadael Moscow. Codi pac a dal y bws ger y farced i fynd i aros 'da Tada a Nana am wylie prin. O'n i ar bigau'r drain pob cam o'r ffordd. Heibio'r ysgol, heibio'r ysbyty, y tai crand gyda gerddi mawr, ac allan… Allan i'r awyr iach a'r cefn gwlad.

Roedd 'yn nhadcu a'n famgu'n ffermio darn o dir ar gyrion y ddinas. Roedd y tyddyn yn gartre' perffeth i fachgen o'r ddinas gyda 'dychymyg bywiog'. Roedd cant a mil o bethe i'w gwneud yno. Angenfilod i'w maeddu. Mynyddoedd i'w darganfod. Moroedd i'w nofio. Ac ar ôl cinio roedd rhaid i rywyn fwydo Bwtch yr afr hefyd.

'Dere 'da fi nawr, Cyw. Ma' ishe casglu'r wyau.'

Bob bore fydde Nana'n gofyn am 'yn help i gasglu'r wyau. Roedd dwylo'r ddau ohonon ni'n ddigon bach i estyn i mewn i'r cwb a dwyn y wyau bychain twym heb ormod o drafferth.

O'n i'n dwlu ar bob un o'r ieir oedd yn dodwy i Nana. O'n i wrth 'y modd yn eu gwylio nhw'n cerdded ar hyd y buarth am orie hir. Yn dychmygu beth yn gwmws o'n nhw'n 'i weud wrth 'i gilydd… clwc, clwc… pa gynllwyniau o'n nhw'n creu… clwc clwc… a'r clecs o'n nhw'n hel tra'n cerdded i fyny ac i lawr eu milltir sgwar.

Eira o'dd 'yn ffefryn. Iâr fawr ddu oedd yn f'atgoffa i o'r fenyw o'dd yn darllen y newyddion ar y teledu bob nos. Eira o'dd bós y teulu bach o ieir. Y frenhines. Y brifathrawes. Y don. Eira o'dd yr un i arwain y ffordd bob tro, i dorri dadl ac i warchod y cywion bychain rhag y cathod o'dd yn byw yn y sgubor.

Gwybodus, caredig, teg… Roedd Eira'n berffeth. 'Nana? Wyt ti'n caru Eira cymaint ag ydw i?' Edrychodd Nana arno i'n dwp. 'Cyw…? Pam fydde rhywun yn caru iâr?'

Y noson cyn i ni ddychwelyd i Foscow, wnaeth Nana baratoi swper arbennig i ni. Roedd y cig yn dyner ac yn flasus.

Y bore trannoeth sylwes i fod Eira 'di diflannu.

Lefes i'r holl ffordd adre.

RHAN II

'Dwi'n dweud 'tho ti, Cyw. Ti'n mynd i newid y byd rhyw ddydd.'

Roedd ymgyrchwyr 'di bod yn annog pobol i gymryd rhan yn y brotest ers dyddie. Roedd Blodyn wedi clywed bod Cadno – pishyn o'dd e 'di bod yn cwrso heb unrhyw lwc o gwbwl ers wthnose – yn mynd i fod yno. Felly, o'dd yn rhaid i ni fynd 'fyd.

Hon o'dd 'y mhrotest gynta' i. Wthnos yn gynharach oedd y Maer 'di canslo'r Orymdaith Pride. Yr orymdaith gynta' o'i math yn y ddinas. O'n i 'di clywed si bod carfan o bobol yn bwriadu cyflwyno deiseb yn ymbil arno fe i ail-ystyried. Ond o'n i ddim 'di bwriadu ymuno â nhw nes bod Blodyn 'di erfyn arno i i gadw cwmni iddo.

Doedd dim sôn am Cadno pan gyrhaeddon ni'r man ymgynnull. Dim ond rhyw hanner cant ohonon ni o'dd wedi mentro allan i wneud safiad.

O'n ffenest ar y degfed llawr o'n i 'di dychmygu byddin o ddynion hoyw a lesbiaid yn cerdded strydoedd Moscow yn swyno'r mwyafrif o'dd yn ein casau ni. Dim byddin. Llond bỳs, falle.

Roedd y newyddion bod criw o cwiars yn bwriadu galw ar y Maer 'di teithio'n bell... O'r 'stafelloedd bychain lle o'n i a'n ffrindie'n mynd i ddawnsio bob nos Sadwrn i 'stafelloedd byw teuluoedd parchus. O ganlyniad, roedd cynulleidfa fawr 'di ymgynnull i'n croesawu ni. Ond nid cynulleidfa gyfeillgar oedd hon. Ac i brofi hynny, wnaeth un neu ddau ohonyn nhw ddangos 'u dannedd.

Chwythodd y gwynt yn gryf.

Wrth i ni gerdded, dechreuodd y gynulleidfa gweiddi enwau. Wnes i ddal llaw Blodyn yn dynn. Gweiddodd y gynulleidfa'n uwch. Roedd pobol o bob lliw a llun wedi dod i'n sarhau ni. Dynion ifanc, gwragedd tŷ, plant ysgol, a'r heddlu… ond yn y rhes flaen o'dd criw o hen fenywod… ac oedd 'da phob un ohonyn nhw fasged.

Roedd Nana 'di defnyddio basged debyg ar y fferm… basged i gasglu…

Cododd un hen fenyw 'i braich…

Edryches i lan i'r nefoedd a dechreuodd e fwrw… wyau.

Darodd yr wy gynta' Blodyn ar 'i ysgwydd. Gwympodd yr ail wrth 'y nhraed. Roedd yr wyau'n cwympo fel arfau o awyren yn hedfan uwch ein penne.

Bang! Games i i'r chwith… Bang! Symudes i i'r dde… Bang! Jwmpes i i fyny. Bang! O'n i'n symud i bob cyfeiriad i osgoi cael 'y mwrw. Edrychodd Blodyn arno i. 'Hei! Mae Cyw yn dawnsio! Dawnsio!' Ac fe o'n i. O'n i'n dawnsio fel o'n i'n dawnsio bob nos Sadwrn gyda'n ffrindie – 'y nghariadon – y bobol ddewr o'dd yn gwrthod cuddio.

Roedd y gerddoriaeth yn uchel. Uchel a phrydferth. Mor brydferth wnaeth y gerddoriaeth ddwyn perswâd ar Blodyn a'r lleill i ddechre dawnsio hefyd. Dawnsio a dawnsio, a wyau'r hen fenywod yn cwympo o'n cwmpas ni fel glaw mawr melyn.

Yna, daeth y dyrne, dyrne'r dynion gyda'r penne moel… Bang! Bang! Daeth y dawnsio i ben.

* * *

O ffenest yr ysbyty, ar y degfed llawr, weles i deigrod yn chwarae yn y caeau, draig yn nofio yn yr afon, ac ieir prydferth yn hedfan drwy'r cymyle.

Roedd yr awyr yn las.